DISCOVER MY WORLD

out and about

First edition for the United States and Canada published by Barron's Educational Series, Inc., 1995

Original title of the book in Spanish: *DESCUBRO MI MUNDO*: LAS EXCURSIONES
© Copyright PARRAMÓN EDICIONES, S.A. 1995
Published by Parramón Ediciones, S.A., Barcelona, Spain.

Authors: Carme Llonch and Laura Blanco
Illustrators: María Rius and Bartolomé Seguí
English text: © Copyright 1995 by Barron's Educational Series, Inc.

All inquiries should be addressed to:
Barron's Educational Series, Inc.
250 Wireless Boulevard
Hauppauge, New York 11788

Library of Congress Catalog Card No. 95-15148

International Standard Book No. 0-8120-6529-8

Library of Congress Cataloging-in-Publication Data
Llonch, Carme.
    [Excursiones. English]
    Out and about / [authors: Carme Llonch and Laura Blanco ;
    illustrators: María Rius and Bartolomé Seguí].
        p.   cm. — (Discover my world)
    Summary: A rhyming trip to the country, city, the seashore,
and the mountains with activities suited to each region.
    ISBN 0-8120-6529-8
    1. Geography—Juvenile literature   [1. Geography]   I. Blanco,
Laura, ill.   II. Rius, María, ill.   III. Seguí, Bartolomé.
IV. Title.   V. Series: Descubro mi mundo.   English.
G133.L5613   1995
910—dc20   95-15148
                                        CIP
                                        AC

PRINTED IN SPAIN
567 9960 987654321

Out and about

in the country

Here in the country you're certain to find
fruit trees of every description and kind;

Here in the country it's peaceful and green,
let's take a walk and you'll see what I mean.

Rumbling tractors are plowing the land,
turning and churning the dirt with their blades;
Sometimes the farmer plants seedlings by hand,

Forming the seed rows with shovels and spades.
One day, one fun day, the seeds will all sprout;
it's so exciting to see what comes out.

What happens
to seeds?

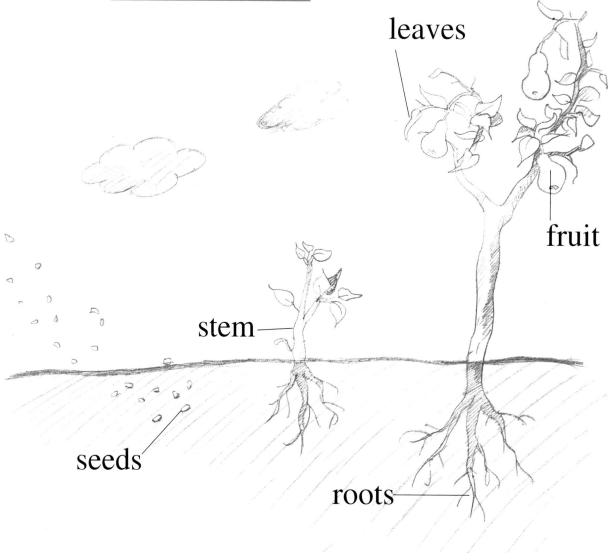

leaves

fruit

stem

seeds

roots

Sunflowers smile at the sun in the morning,
bask in the glow of it all afternoon;
Sunflowers never grow tired of sunshine,
blooming all summer, beginning in June.

Here in the country you're bound to see fruit trees heavy with cherries, delicious and sweet.
Up in the trees you are sure to see blackbirds,

helping themselves to a midsummer treat,

Gobbling down all those tasty red cherries,
pecking away at them, bit by small bit,
leaving behind just the stone in the center—
everyone knows that you can't eat a pit!

Do you know
these fruits?

an apple

a banana

a peach

a melon

strawberries

an orange

Here in the country the fruits that you see
soon will be harvested fresh from the tree,
packed into boxes and big wooden crates,
shipped to the markets in faraway states.

Look at the vegetables, leafy and green,
round heads of lettuce, the biggest you've seen;

Heavy bell peppers that cling to the vine,
drooping tomato plants tied up with twine.

Here in the country the geese and the ducks
never get scared by the fast roaring trucks;
Safely they cross the road all in a row,
here in the country the traffic is slow.

Here in the country some chicks have been born,
hungry red hens peck at kernels of corn,
floppy eared rabbits are snug in their hutch,
nibbling lettuce they like very much.

Listen, listen, can you hear them?
Grunting piglets, you're right near them;
In the meadow cows are mooing,
munching grasses, softly chewing.

In the meadow golden grasses
ripen as the season passes;
One day soon the blooms will die
underneath a changing sky.

Now the snow has covered over
all the fields of rye and clover;

Even though the warmth has gone,
life, of course, still carries on.

Guess what I am:
I am found on a vine;
When I am crushed
I am fruit juice or wine;
Sometimes I'm green,
I'm purple, or red;
Dry me and try me as
raisins instead.

Out and about

Out and about

in the city

Look at the city! How big and exciting!
Buildings and parks are so grand and inviting.

Statues, museums, and skyscrapers call;
Let's go exploring—we'll visit them all.

So many houses, they're making me dizzy;
Who would have thought that the streets were so busy?

Hundreds of buildings that reach to the sky;
How can they live in apartments that high?

What a crowded shopping center!
Let's find out where we can enter.
Look at all the suits and ties;
Gee, I hope they have my size.

I just love that big blue sweater!
Wait. . . I like the green one better.
City stores are so much fun;
Something here for everyone.

Out and about

What do they sell
in these shops?

the butcher

the drugstore

the bakery

the florist

the bookstore

Good things to eat are for sale in the street;
Open air vendors have set up their stands.
Buy a carnation, a new publication,
a snack in a sack you can eat with your hands.

Traffic roaring, hear the rumble;
Side streets, cross streets, what a jumble!

Screeching taxis, motor scooters,
trucks with angry horn toot tooters;
Stop and go, you can't get far,
and still no place to park your car.

Do you know what noises a car, a motorcycle, an ambulance, and a bicycle make?

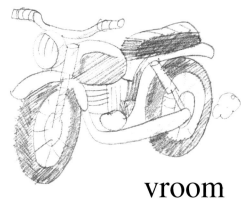

vroom
a motorcycle

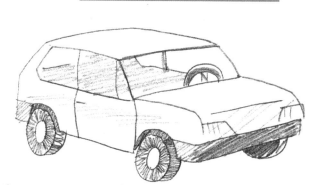

brrrrr
a car

weeEE-weeEE
an ambulance

ring-ring
a bicycle

Going and coming, the city is humming,
clanging and banging, alive and awake;
Headlights are glaring and sirens are blaring;
Oh, what a terrible racket they make!

Trains can take us all around,
subway riding underground;
Signs will help us make connections,
maps will give us clear directions;

We will see historic places,
statues with their stony faces.
Won't you take my picture, please?
Hold the camera, I'll say "Cheese!"

So many people, but no one we know;
All of them strangers with places to go.
Late for appointments with no time to talk;
Look how determined, how quickly they walk.

Here in the park it's a much different place;
Everyone moves at a nice easy pace.
Kids can ride bicycles, buy a balloon,
stroll in the shade on a warm afternoon.

Slowly a lowering sun cools the town;
Just for a moment, the city slows down.
Offices close at the end of the day;
Buses and trains carry workers away.

Now in the night all the storefronts are bright;
Streets are awash in the wild neon light.
This is the city, it's leaving its mark,
just like a diamond, it shines in the dark.

Guess what I am:
I'm a city's delight.
The stories I tell
are what give me my height.
I'm not a threat
to the skies that I scrape;
Without me, the skyline
would not have a shape.

Out and about

Out and about

at the seashore

Rolling and crashing, the waves never stop,
turning and churning with whitecaps on top;

Rising and falling in furious fun,
melting to foam at the end of their run.

Snowy white seagulls fly over the ocean,
looking for fish they can swoop down and snatch;

Sharp-eyed, they watch for the tiniest motion,
some fish are not quite so easy to catch.

Out and about

What sails on
the sea?

a submarine

a waterjet

a speedboat

a pedal-boat

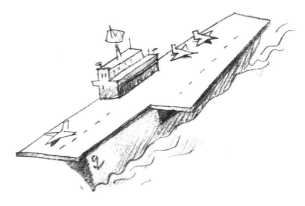

an aircraft carrier

Sailboats are blown by the wind on the water,
powered by breezes that push them along.
Sailing a sailboat is certainly tricky;
Sailors have got to be nimble and strong.

Look at this steamship, it's carrying people.
Look at the people, they're crowding the decks,

Waving to us in our little red rowboat,
so far away that we're nothing but specks.

Yo ho ho we sit on ropes,
watching through our telescopes;
I can see for miles and miles,
all the way to distant isles.

Golden beaches in the sun,
swimmers having lots of fun;
Some are in a paddleboat,
some are just content to float.

Isn't it grand just to play in the sand
and jump in the waves as they break on the land?

Under the shade an umbrella has made
it's fun to relax with a cool lemonade.

What would you take to the beach?

a bathing suit

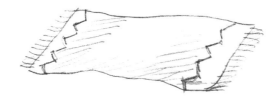

a towel

sunscreen

a bucket

an umbrella

a shovel

Boats are arriving with flounder and trout,
bringing the catch of the day;
Some of the big fish are flopping about,
trying to wriggle away.

Evening falls, it's eight o'clock.
The fishing boats are at the dock,
back in port, securely tied
and bobbing gently, side by side.

Back again on native shores
the fishermen have many chores;
Even as a red sun sets,
they're hard at work repairing nets.

I'm oh so very curious:
What makes the sea so furious
to crash against the rocks like that
and smash thc reeds and seashells flat—

When in the depths so cool and green,
the sea is silent and serene?
How marvelous it seems to me
how many things the sea can be.

Guess what I am:
I have rudders and sails;
I don't weigh or measure,
although I have scales;
I might be an angel,
a devil, a king,
a cat without claws,
a guitar with no string.

Out and about

Out and about

in the mountains

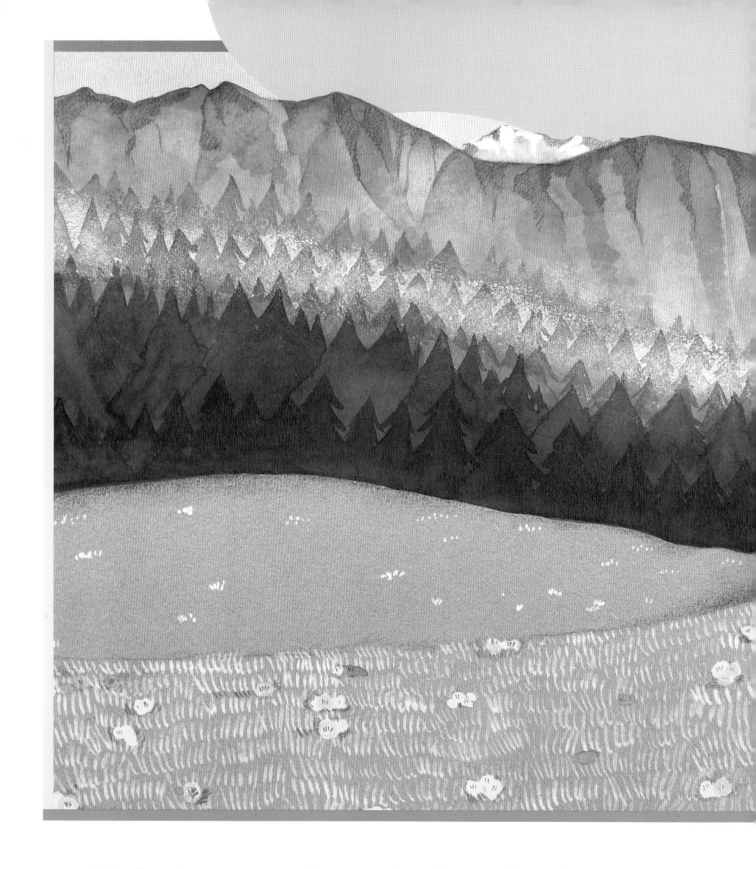

Up in the mountains so far from the city
the forests and meadows are peaceful and pretty;

Up in the mountains we'll sleep in a tent
while cornflowers perfume the air with their scent.

Quaint little villages sit in the valleys;
Steeple bells ring in the clear mountain air.

Look at the buttercups dotting the hillside.
Wouldn't you like to go picnicking there?

Trails in the mountains are narrow and shady,
scattered with mushrooms and covered with leaves;

Shy summer strawberries grow in the shadows,
kissed by the rainfall the forest receives.

Out and about

What would you
wear to go walking
in the mountains?

a backpack

boots

a hat

a canteen

binoculars

Hiking's a snap if you've got a good map—
you'll never, no never get lost;
There's no need to fear, you can see we're right here—
The place where these two roads have crossed.

This is a spot that I come to a lot,
the scenery here is so grand;

The valley below was formed long, long ago
when glaciers moved over the land.

Look at the eagles, we're lucky to see them.
Look at them soaring! I wish we could be them.
I can see deer, but I don't think they'll stay;
Something, I guess, must have scared them away.

Here in the mountains the waterfalls tumble,
carrying bits of the rocks that they crumble;
Maybe you shouldn't climb onto that bar—
you could slip off if you lean in too far.

People may say that the lakes are like ice,
too cold for wading, but I think they're nice;
Slow melting snow from the previous year
keeps the lake chilly but naturally clear.

Up here the landscape is rugged and bare,
trees can't survive in the thin mountain air;
Still, there is beauty in being so high,
far from the foothills but close to the sky.

Do you know
what the parts
of a mountain
are called?

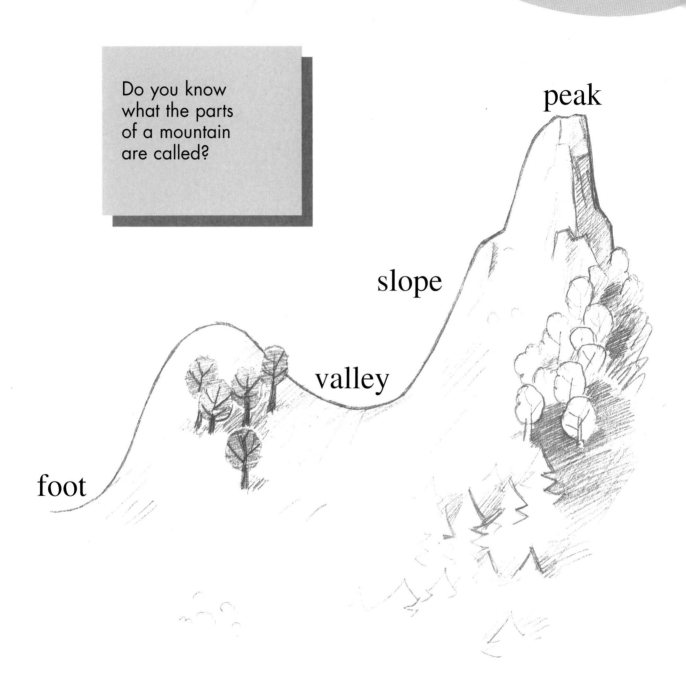

peak

slope

valley

foot

Snow in the mountains! The skiers are ready,
trying to hold themselves upright and steady,
sliding and gliding for hours and hours,
over the ski trails where once there were flowers.

85

Wind in the mountains can howl through the clover, rustle the branches and topple you over;

Sun in the mountains can color your cheeks,
melt all the snow on the tall mountain peaks.

Guess what I am:
I am never at rest;
As long as I'm falling,
I'm doing my best;
Though gravity pulls me,
I make my own course;
Snow that melts down
is my primary source.

IN THE CITY

The following fun activities will help bring children closer to some of the subjects that have appeared in this book. Parental supervision is required.

How to make jigsaw puzzles out of postcards.

OBJECTIVE
To recognize shapes and understand continuance.

MATERIALS
Postcards with city scenes, paint, a paintbrush, scissors, and a shoebox

WHAT TO DO
- Paint the back of each postcard in a solid color. Use a different color for each postcard.
- Cut each postcard into eight pieces. Make the pieces different shapes and sizes.
- Try to put the pieces back together again to

form the scene on the postcard. The pieces with the same color backs belong to the same scene.

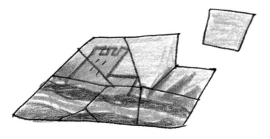

- Keep the postcard puzzles in a shoebox.

How to make a magnetic game

OBJECTIVE
To develop coordination and accuracy of movement.

MATERIALS

Drawing paper, felt tip markers, glue, a shoebox, a magnet, corks, and metal thumbtacks.

WHAT TO DO

- Cut a piece of paper the same size as one of the long sides of the shoebox.

- Draw a city map on the paper. Draw wide roads, big streets, and city buildings along the streets.

- Turn the shoebox on its side and glue the map to the opposite side.

- Draw people and cars on another piece of paper.

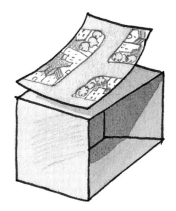

At the bottom of each one, add a little tab. Cut them out.

- Fold back the tabs and glue the bottom of each one to the top of a cork so that your cars and people are "standing" on the corks.

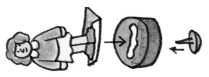

- Stick a thumbtack all the way into the bottom of each cork.

- Turn the shoebox on its side. Place your cars along the roads on the map. Place the people on the streets & sidewalks.

- Slide the magnet along the inside of the shoebox close to the map side. The magnet will pull the thumbtacks. Try to make the people and cars move along the streets by moving the magnet.

AT THE SEASHORE

How to make a necklace

MATERIALS
Seashells, string, and a plastic bag.

WHAT TO DO
• Collect some small seashells when you go to the beach. Look for shells that have one or two tiny holes in them. Keep the shells in a plastic bag. Rinse off the shells when you get home.

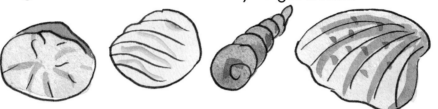

• Cut a length of string long enough for a necklace.

• Thread the shells onto the string and tie the ends together.

How to play hopscotch

WHAT TO DO

OBJECTIVE
To develop coordination of movements and a sense of balance.

- Draw this hopscotch grid on the sand and number the boxes as shown. Make the boxes big enough to stand in.

- Choose who will go first, second, and so on.

- Stand in front of the grid and try to toss a pebble into Box 1 without having it land on any of the lines.

- Skip Box 1 and hop on one foot directly to Box 2. If you step on a line, you're out.

- From Box 2, hop to Box 3. Jump to Boxes 4 and 5 at the same time, putting one foot in each box. Hop to Box 6 and then to 7. Then jump to Boxes 8 and 9, putting one foot in each box.

- Jump to the rest area, turn around, and go back the same way.

- When you get to Box 2, before you leave the hopscotch, pick up the pebble without stepping in Box 1. Jump over Box 1 and off the grid.

- Now, toss the pebble into Box 2. Repeat the trip, this time skipping Box 2. Always skip the box with the pebble.

- Your turn ends if you step on a line or miss the toss.

IN THE MOUNTAINS

How to play four corners

RULES OF THE GAME

- This game is for five players.
- Select four trees that form a big square.
- One player stands in the middle of the square, and the others each stand against a different tree.

- When the player in the middle says, "One, two, three, four corners," everyone must change trees. The player in the middle tries to get to a tree too. Whoever doesn't get to a tree becomes the player in the middle.

How to make a greeting card

MATERIALS

Paint, cardboard, scissors, an old toothbrush, dry leaves, and a newspaper.

WHAT TO DO

- Spread the newspaper over your work area.
- Cut a piece of cardboard in the shape of a rectangle and fold it in half. This will be your greeting card.
- Place a leaf on the cover of your card.

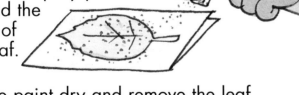

- Dip the bristles of the toothbrush into some paint. Let most of the paint drip back into the jar.
- Hold the toothbrush over the edges of the leaf and run your finger across the bristles to spray paint around the edge of the leaf.

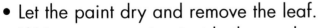

- Let the paint dry and remove the leaf.
- Write your greeting inside the card.

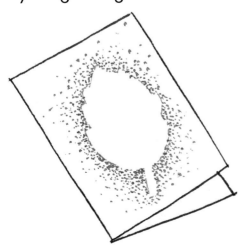

How to make strawberry jam

MATERIALS
Jars with lids, a large pot, a hand mixer, and labels.

INGREDIENTS:
2 lbs (1 kg) fresh strawberries, 3 ¼ cups (750 g) sugar, juice from 1 lemon, 1 cup water

WHAT TO DO
- Wash the strawberries, remove the leaves, and put them in a pot with the sugar.
- Add the lemon juice and the water.
- Cook the strawberries uncovered over a low heat for about 25 minutes, stirring occasionally.

- Remove the pot from the stove and beat the mixture with a hand mixer until it is smooth. Return the pot to the stove and allow it to cook another 5 minutes.

- Fill the jars with the jam and allow them to cool. Cover the jars and label each one with the date.

- Keep the jam in the refrigerator. Always check the jam before you eat it. Fresh jam can spoil very quickly.